Praise for

'A book of poems for the walkers and dreamers, for those people who step outside and pay attention to the 'dreaming world' which -in the author's lovely words is 'present as wind.''

~ Jane Yolen, author of over 400 books for children and adults

'These poems take us far away from the deadly mechanisms of modernity and into the deeply eloquent lifeways of our animate earth. They open doorways into the forgotten realm of nature's soul which we so deeply need to rediscover in this time of crisis.'

~ Stephan Harding, author of Animate Earth and Gaia Alchemy

'Sometimes the beings of our world will tell you who they are, if you listen. The world comes alive and you know you are being seen. These fine poems are a record of such a remarkable event. Take them seriously. Let them guide you into that open field.'

~ Tom Cheetham, author of Boundary Violations and other books

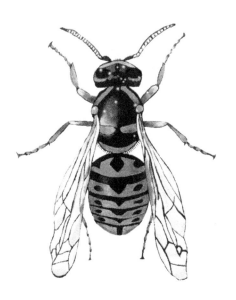

Copyright © 2022 by Ben Patrick Holden

www.benpholden.com

British Library Cataloguing in Publication Data

Vespers

First published in 2022

A CIP catalogue record of this book is
available from the British Library

Cover painting by Lisa Jane Kilty
Copyright © 2022 LJK
www.lisakilty.co.uk

ISBN 9798449101709

For Carol Mary Holden

Mother

Poet

Pirate

Contents

Introduction

Not long ago I was seized by the unsettling realisation that I am nowhere near as awake to the world as I once was, or would like to be again.

In the liminal realm of childhood a thousand faerie streams flow into us on a daily basis, every little experience crackling with vibrancy. The world is shudderingly alive for a time, then we grow up, and it stops speaking to us in the same way.

There's something about our culture that encourages an ossification of the senses and a blindness to awe. That luminous topology of imagination gets squeezed and flattened, the spired towers and labyrinthine castles of the child's inner world are replaced by the dull res extensa of motorways, computer screens and office blocks that come to dominate our localities and the imaginal worlds those localities are interanimated with.

The world was once a living body replete with secrets, every glowing cloud and sleeping stone a fellow presence enfolded within the great community of being. Now it's often camera fodder, the setting sun snapped into our smartphones before we've felt the kiss of its light.

When the cosmos continued its relentless tumble of violent creativity by coagulating some of its physical and invisible substance into the being known as 'Ben', it did so by granting a fistful of blessings which gave me a fighter's chance of keeping those faerie streams alive.

Some of these blessings were family-shaped; a mother who, in her teens, wandered around Manchester in an elven cloak reciting William Butler Yates, and a father afflicted with so much creative hutzpah that founding and performing in a travelling circus was just one in a string of outrageous high-wire acts.

The cavalcade of unconventional characters surrounding my early life included all sorts of misfits and weirdos, green witches and hedge wizards, a lot of them contained within the sheltering walls of Hebden Bridge, a village now as famed for its artists and gay folk as it is for its flooding. There, at the Bronte end of the South Pennines, a shamble away from the place Ted Hughes entered the fray, I went about my merry business, quietly assuming the whole world was like Hebden.

It wasn't, and after thirty odd years of moving through this broken, glorious mess, the world at large managed to loop its tendrils around my daimon's esophagus. But the attempted suffocation failed, and that invisible twin who guides the trajectory of these sentences is coming back, swinging.

Exaggeration is vital here, mainly because the soul-eroding effects of the world at large are so pervasive, so ingrained in our ways of speaking, our habits and institutions, that a certain amount of spirited language is required to break the spell. Poetry excells at this, and the poems in this little book exist for that reason.

Writing this book was an accident. It happened gradually, poem by poem. The necessity to keep writing came from the realisation that I'd inadvertently picked up some of the habits and holding patterns of the very thing I was trying to stand against: the world of dry information and mass-produced experiences, hyper-addictive technologies and commerce gone psychotic; a world that facilitates our forgetting and complicity in ecological crisis, whilst damming up the faeries streams so effectively that we can barely hear the trickle of the anima mundi's bleeding heart.

When a civilisation treats its citizens more like machine parts than co-creators blessed with a divine spark, then that civilisation's children are going to be broken in all kinds of ways. Fathers will be absent, mothers compromised. The demons in the culture will find their way into the homes of families, running havoc in the psyche, making wounds in the soul. With no lens or language to see them or name them, these demons inhabit family lines just as freely as they inhabit the culture's past and the stories that have brought us here. The gods are dead and we hold the knife, Nizche says. Regardless of how much truth that holds, there is a wound in the heart of our culture - a longing that makes itself known when we turn off the screen. How long can you stand the silence before reaching for your phone?

But imagine a culture in which it was normal to grow up feeling deeply welcome and witnessed, as if your surrounding community and its institutions cared deeply about who you are and what you might become. We don't have that, and in the absence of true blessings we seek 'external validation', to use the language of the times, often through AI-backed social media platforms explicitly designed to capture and monetize our attention.

These poems are an attempt to clothe myself in wild language for the sake of sanity, truth, and beauty. Language can either shut down or open up the faerie streams that keep us linked to the soul of the world. In a culture where our ways of speaking often feel as tame and square as the built environments we inhabit, poetry becomes vital. It's a way of stitching ourselves a protective cloak - a kind of soul armour. All we have to do is read it, and if we dare, write it.

I hope a few of these poems are alive enough to become threads in your own cloak. Perhaps you've been stitching one for longer than you realise, or perhaps it's well-worn already and just needs a little repair. Either way, may it keep you safe in the storms ahead.

Ben Patrick Holden

'Vesper' – Definitions

1. A late afternoon or evening worship

2. A planet, usually Venus, seen at sunset in the western sky

3. Wasp

Vespers

Wasp clings on a mountain cairn
collecting silver
droplets
from the mist.

We camped here once,
my dad and I;
son and father, mountain top,
washed in starlight on the cairn.

Were we collecting silver then?

Now the only stars
have gathered on the wasp;
constellated Queens and Kings
and the bone-white gaze of Jesters.

The chapels are in disrepair,
Venus washed out by the mist.
My company; a dying wasp
and the wind that sings his vespers.

Forgotten as a Breath

When satellites bisect the stars,
when drones dissect the sky,
when the deepest cave in Earth is mapped,
where can I go
to find the words
to speak a prayer
for the other world?
That dreaming world,
patient as soil,
present as wind,
forgotten as a breath.

Imagination

Imagination
is not housed inside your skull.

Your skull
and its lovely brain
shares a home with your heart.
Your body,
with its lively blood,
lives inside the world;
this home of earth,
sky,
falling water,
and fire in the mind.

Imagination
does not live only inside you.
You live inside
Imagination.

Kingfisher

Kingfisher,
tell me how
to plummet with such grace
into cold and darkness
beneath the river's rippling face.

Kingfisher,
tell me how
to hunt inside the dark,
alone inside the river's chest,
called to a silver spark.

Kingfisher,
tell me how
to seek beauty in the dark,
like Psyche with her silver key,
a gift from lost Persephone.

Kingfisher,
tell me how
to grace the gray of day,
to dress as if the gods were watching,
and live the diver's way.

Being Breathed

I watch my son
breathing in his sleep,
kept alive
and kept alive
by a presence all about us,
filling up his little lungs,
flowing steady through his blood,
a steady gift,
steady given,
every moment
of my life
and his.

Magicians of the Woods

Moth sleeps inside
the hagwood of a trunk
dreaming of the kingtree
in whose body she is sunk.

Hornet drinks the brew
moving through the oak,
from a cleft in the root
spills the hidden yolk.

Beetle walks the labyrinth,
oak leaves red as rust,
shakes the scepter in his claw;
the labyrinth turns to dust.

Second Skin

Cast off the dross!
All the plastic thoughts
and anesthetic words.

Shiver!
like the polar bear
shaking off the ice.

Slide!
like the earthworm
in a sleeve of silver dirt.

Shimmer!
like the octopus
in a shirt of mottled shells.

Scavenge!
like the magpie,
a nest of shining secrets.

Let this be your second skin
to keep you safe
from pale culture
and speech grown thin.

Glass Prison

I wish to escape the Glass Prison
but the wish,
being wished within its walls,
is turned to glass.

The wall of the Glass Prison
are millennia thick
and no one knows where they are.
A woman found them once,
touched them,
but her hands to glass.
She could no longer feel.

The air of the Glass Prison is pale.
Words spoken into it
are drained of colour
and quickly forget how to fly.

Some say a child's touch
could turn the walls to water,
but every day the children are fed
spoonfuls of glass soup
making them think glassy thoughts,
speak glassy words
learned from a glass curriculum
in schools of glass
from a glass government,
its glass ministers
breathing the same glassy air
as the glass poets and glass painters,
the glass rebels and glass revolutionaries,
all held within
the walls of the Glass Prison.

Spectre

Your senses,
so bright as a child,
now tenuous things,
there one moment
gone the next.

Touch,
the one you miss most,
returns briefly
and you feel the wind
on your spectral clothes
as if they were your naked skin
and a great longing comes over you—
to be part of the physical once more;
the familial world
that all weighted things share;
the juggling ball,
the boy who throws it,
the ground that supports him,
the moon that moves the tides around him.

Gods,
grant me the courage
to live
as if I was alive.

The Longest Work

I gather limbs of oak and alder,
lash them tight with marsh reeds
then begin the longest work
of holding up the frame.
Tilted at an oblique angle
in the darkest stretch of forest,
not a frame for any vine
but a trellis
for spirits to climb.

Silence on Queen's Crag

There I stood upon the crag,
head bowed to buried Queens
when on the reaching winter wind
came the braying of a stag.

Staring down from on the hill,
without a turn, without a start,
his body still as sleeping stones,
his eyes an arrow in the heart.

There we stood in ancient light,
the day moon hidden now from sight,
the winter sun still hanging low,
making shadows with the crags,
painting faces on the stones,
faces witnessed once by kings,
kings with faces carved in stone,
touched by self-same winter sun.

Gone the meadows.
Gone the oaks.
Gone the salmon in the streams.
Gone the footprints of the wolves.
Gone their hackled hoar-frost dreams.

Then the stag turned his head
to where a forlorn farmhouse stood,
banked by a meager copse of pine

where a three-finned tower milled the wind.

Not a single road.
Not a single wire.
Not a single sign of smoking fire.

Only stillness;
a watching man,
a watching stag.

To Kill a Fly with Divine Beauty

Today I killed a fly,

squashed it on the window

with 'Divine Beauty' by John O'Donohue.

I opened the book,

spoke a line a random.

'Beauty itself is a profound invitation to a new kind of knowing.'

Is the dead fly beautiful?

Is the death-smear on the window?

Behind me stands a small bronze statue:

Aphrodite

leaning into a sun beam.

Just as the fly did

when it followed the eddies into my shed,

tasting my salts in the air.

There are other flies still buzzing.

I could grab the statue and take them out too.

Me and Aphrodite,

make a death-smear constellation,

place her in its centre,

paint her face with their juices,

sing her a dead-fly song,

give her a dead-fly dance

as she laughs,

beautifully,

at my efforts

to salvage beauty in their deaths.

Night Wind

I like it when the night wind blows,
cold crashing through the trees,
crashing cold through oak and ash,
coaxing pines to sway and lash.

I like the seething song they sing
that turns the mind to sky,
that douses out all dreary thought
and blasts away the dross.

But most of all I like the sound
of trickling silver in the dark,
buried under miles of wind,
a vein of water makes it mark.

Down beneath the shivered leaves
lives the sound that I like best,
beside her banks I listen—
to the hidden jewel in the valley's chest.

No Name Will Do

If names have power
then what name
could possibly hold
this world,
this home ,
this ancient glowing orb,
grown in the womb of impossible cosmos.

'Earth' will not do it.
'Gaia' will not do it.
'World' falls flat in the mind.

Perhaps only silence
can speak,
so bow
to stars,
soil,
rains,

and be filled
with hidden names.

Green Gold Light

I'm a hunter for the green gold light
that spills through leaves,
plunges through rivers,
draping itself in the eddies of boulders
and the gliding shadows of clover,
bursting out
in veins of shimmering crystal
and shoals of green-gold salmon,
brushing their translucent bellies
over the branches, leaves and cheeks
of all the lifted faces
swaying in their graces.

Not a Machine

You are not a flat tire.
You are not a broken engine.
You are not a servo whose battery needs replacing.
You are not a computer whose software needs updating.

If someone whispers in your ear everyday:
'Did you know you're a machine?'
you're likely to believe it.
But if you're heart is a chambered pump
then its full of kingfishers,
hundreds of them,
calling to the vast herds of oxen
stampeding through your blood,
and the boars in your belly
sniffing about for chunks of starlight
and bulbs of roasted gold.

You are not a machine.

You are a communion of creatures,
a cavalcade of critters
tossing around champagne,
lashing magma coloured bunting
across the balconies of your brain.
Descendants of bacteria
drunk on raven speech and heron call,
throwing chemical poetry through your cells,
like contraband cast over the Berlin wall;

Premium Moonshine,
Dionysian Red,
fermented in the cellars of Kronos,
spilling forth divine inspiration
that moves the hand
of Marie Curie and Mary S. Morgan,
of Miles Davis and Charles Darwin,
of Anne Conway and Da Vinci's left.

So break the seal on the WD40
and remember
that it's time to get naughty
with the hundred thousand mysteries
twisting
and listing
on the shining, gleaming, golden edge
of your darkly shadowed vision.

Floating World

In the valley steeps,
outside Trixie's place,
we gather round a battered wooden table
for my brother's thirty third.

In this town of water mills,
of acid trips and juggling balls,
of lost souls and crystal cults,
and hidden graveyards in the hills.

We feast on sashimi and tempura,
bought on the dregs of meager savings
as April snow dissolves in our sake,
we reminisce
on Tokyo
and the Floating World.

Memories of sakura petals peeling
through the backstreets of Shinjuku,
the city's night air
burning red with neon glyphs,
alive with the gusting brush of kami
riding the sky to courtyard shrines.

In our village of canalways and cobblestones,
of ley lines and bricklayers,
of sagging walls and leaning homes,
of bright-eyed kids and miller's bones,
we fill our cups
and say a prayer
for the spirits
swimming in the air.

Anchor

The concrete high-rise in your chest
wants to fall
and fall
and fall.
And will, if you let it;
a high-rise turned to water,
a giant's lance
hurling itself ever into the earth,
so immense in its being
that it shatters all scales,
implodes all measurements,
plunging deeper into Gaia's chest;
an impossible anchor,
impossibly strong,
holding your animal heart
to the ancient heart of the world.

Lead Poison

If you are a dream-boat
or any kind of drifter
then you might want to consider
a prayer or two to Saturn,
that limp-legged old man
standing at the limit of all things,
watching your efforts spill out
through holes in a leaky vessel.

But if you pray to Saturn for guidance
don't be surprised when he delivers
not the loving discipline of an old mentor,
but a spike pushed through your chest
and the long the lead poison to follow.

Do not get defensive.
Do not make your case.
Just listen
and let the wounding do its work.

Village of a Thousand Hidden Streams

My son lay sleeping
a stone's throw
from the place I entered this world:
The Village of a Thousand Hidden Streams.
As my wife sang in the shower
I walked the steeps and ginnels
and I don't know if it was the afterglow
of trying to spark another life
or the bottle of spirits
I'd shared with my brother the night before,
but the village,
in its verticality,
seemed more than itself,
touched by another world,
like the mountain that remembers
it was once underwater.
During such a time
the tea towels on the washing line seem a lot like prayer flags,
and the ice falling from the April sky
has more in common with apricots than bullets,
and you see
that the dappled slate roofs

are glad for the company of herons

and the wall of the terrace

would turn itself translucent

if it meant the boy inside would get the starlight he needed.

When I found myself in the graveyard,

a lantern burned

by a stone for a miller's daughter

whose life tumbled through this village

more than a hundred years ago.

A direct line of sight between her death place

and my birth place

on the other side of the valley.

How strange to feel her company for the boy I was

all those years ago,

kicking stones up the street,

watched over by the grave of a miller's daughter;

two strangers,

their distant fires

giving mutual comfort

from afar.

You Are Here

Sprint through fields, eyes closed.
Pull down spears of ice from the sky,
send them blazing into chasms.
Patch your skeleton with silver mud and salmon flesh,
go dancing in the city of the dead.
Build a walled garden around your heart
with a hundred hidden doors.
Throw a party for the exiled ones,
invite them to stay the night.
Know the mysteries of water are present
in the one who does the dishes.
Feel the blue heart of the world
pulsing in the eyes of your children,
and know
that for just a while
you are here.

The Way Is Down

White feather curls to earth,
does not catch sunlight,
does not float in the air.
The feather's way is down.

Boulder tips from a crag,
slams the shallow water,
does not roll or split.
The boulder's way is down.

Boy stands on the edge
of an island in the clouds,
smiles like the Mona Lisa.
The boy's way is down.

Bring Me Silence

Bring me silence,
fistfuls of it.
Drop it in the pool
resting in my chest.

Send out the cormorants
to fish for silence.
Pull it from their gullets,
slip it down my throat.

Ask the owl in the oak
what it knows of silence.
Ink her words on my skin,
etch them on my eyelids

Find the blackened fruits of silence,
ferment them in a blackened bottle,
and on the silent blackened bridge
we'll share a glass of silent wine.

Ashes and Wings

Who is this boy
falling from the sky?
What is it that he knows
to smile in such a way?
I see his rippling hair
and the light that flits his lashes.
Do his lips shape a prayer
for his wings or his ashes?

Glyphs on Cellar Doors

She walks the slipways of your sleep,
she walks the bone-pile shore.
She walks the city's arcing streets,
marking glyphs on cellar doors.

Her hands are quick, her heart is slow,
her chalk is mined from the hills of Hel.
The glyphs she draws are never still;
half word, half animal.

'Sing me a song to spill your grief.
Sing loud enough for the sky to hear.
Sing it now, sing it now.
Sing! And give the soil your tears.'

Spirit in the Fence Plank

A leaf shadow spins
on a fence plank in the garden,
crisp and dark,
a momentary slither,
serrated little shield.

Its green bodied twin
hidden in plain sight.
Whoever it is,
an invisible bridge links shadow and leaf.
You could try to sever it,
but to pass your hand between them
would only cause you to be included,
your skin a cup
for the leaf-shaped coolness
spinning on your palm.

I thought spirits lived in old trees
and mountains,
but it turns out
they also live in fence planks.

Old Man in the Stars

I stand upon a stage
and go through the motions
of an old, familiar play,
but floating in the air
is a fold of pale silk.
I take it.
Pull.
The stage falls away.
Swimming in the plenum
of the pulsing, breathing stars,
an old man is beaming,
mischief brimming in his eyes.
In his gaze I am flooded,
as an ocean drinks a house,
by an ancient, bright awareness,
a dream of being dreamed.
He is glad to see me,
pleased I pulled the silk.
In his eyes he knows me.
In mine he knows himself.
It is overwhelming
to be present in this gift.
Old man just grins, says:
'That's right. It was me!'

Aurora

Solar flames,
spat from the mouth of god,
the sun,
as vast in violence as in light,
would turn our world to a fiery hell
were it not for the magic shield
born from arcs of molten iron,
womb-hidden;
an out-flung magnetic field.
Held above our blue-green face
in defiance to solar fury,
turning violence into light,
that graces skies in Northern night.

The Shell I Carry

Sometimes in sleep
I retreat
like a snail defending from attack,
and the shell I carry hardens,
shutting out the dreaming world.
When I wake,
the shell remains;
an unseen spiral
heavy on my back.
Is this why my shoulders ache?
Is this what broke the car's suspension?
Shell,
thank you for guarding me,
but sometimes it's such a weight
to carry all this armour.

So let me bless you, friend,
with oils made from river rocks
and the shed skins of vipers.
May you be a noble sentinel
that knows when to harden
and when to soften.
May your broken horns and bony studs
gleam with starlight when owls call.
May your bumps and runnels
be the blind queen's brail.
May your hardened flesh
know the tears of sons
and the laughter of daughters,
the pressure of fox prints
and the pleasures of water.

Black Snakes

Two black snakes ride the estuary,
side by side.
Suspended, they stay
where fresh water meets the sea.

What kind of boundary keepers are these?
Guardians of the mud flats,
sentinels of the liminal realm,
this dawn-mirror I walk upon,
the psychized earth,
the morphic ground,
unfolding its secrets with every pulling step.

I know this land has no black snakes,
yet there they are, real as my rubber boots.
What are they?
Eels?
Otters?
Stones?

I still don't know,
so I call to Proteus and say:
'Come on. What are those things?'
'Black snakes,' he says,
smiling with half his face.

Cosmos Tumbled

Cosmos tumbled,

dancing through the dark,

cheeks burning at the void's cold press,

her body a dark scream,

scattered with cinders,

the stars,

her children,

their voices singeing,

a song unsealed,

symphonic ringing,

rose, now rising,

to a blazing death,

to die,

reprising.

Night Twin

The lantern she carries
is always turned downward
and the bird in her pocket
who always looks homeward
is the light in the window
of the house on the hillside
who sees you and reaches
across the dark valley
for the place where your heart lives
is lost underwater
the ship of your father
torn down to splinters
the books of your sisters
are bleeding their ink out
the bones of your mother
are hidden by winters

while the graves of the tigers

are gathering voices

to sing out a ghost-song

of a long living violence

the trust that was broken

shines in the gutter

the words of the rivers

still go unspoken

but somewhere,

out beyond the border,

your night twin stands,

lantern in hand,

searching for you

with the same desire

you are searching for her.

The Gold in Your Eyes

To attend;
to lean your soul to another
is the truest gold
we can lend.

The Invisible Market knows this.
It wants your gold
and it knows how to get it;
your precious, fleeting gold,
drawn from your eyes
into the clean, bright interface
of the Invisible Market
like spiders draw blood from flies.

Be careful where you place your eyes.

Odysseus warned his shipmates
but they still untied him,
as they untied me one morning
to lend the Sirens my ears and eyes.

My son played with his train track.
I stared into my phone.

Ah it's alright. He's happy by himself.
But now and then he called to me
'Will you give me a little gold?'

The hidden question went unheard
as I spent myself in the Invisible Market
until a third a time, he whispered
'Don't you want to play?'

I threw away the headphones,
pulled away my gaze,
gathered up a heap of gold
and held it for my son.

He climbed on my knees
and to my complete surprise
reached up to give a kiss,
one for each of my eyes.

Hazel Tree

Tide spills over the field.
Peninsula becomes an island.

Hazel tree is alone.
I alone with it.

You're still alive, old friend,
but look what the years have done to you.
Your body is cracked and withered,
your limbs split and hanging.
But still,
we are both still here.
It is good to see you.

Moon dips,
tide drops.

A bridge appears.
Hazel tree is not alone.

Blue Shield

Somewhere at the edge of the world,
in a castle,
in a forest
by the sea,
a boy floats on a blue shield;
twilight metal
held aloft by his father's word;
the king who stands beneath him,
a father
sailing his son
through the old library
with magic meant for serious things.
Past the buckling shelves
and all across the rafters,
a sacred sound tumbles forth;
the boy's and father's laughter.

A Closing Vesper

One year to shelter trouble and beauty.
One year to embrace decay.
One year to be confused and confounded.
One year to spin a second skin.

Have you ever lain upside-down
to watch the sun slide up into the hills?
Lit from within,
the sky reveals another face,
calling forth your hidden topology.

Suddenly it occurs
that you have not been looking
at the undersides of clouds
but down upon mountains,
snow-crested and glowing,
their slopes swallowed
into the blue expanse
concealing vales and valleys,
passageways and passes
linking long forgotten temples
and unseen cities
whose people stare up at a strange green sky
and wonder who might be looking down.

To emerge from this inversion
is like flipping the sand timer half way through;
earth pours into sky,
sky pours into earth.
Now the long-bodied hills are migrating creatures
in a story unfolding at the pace of your breath.

A simple prayer for a sublime moment.
Thank you for including me.

As I turn to leave
something glints in the western sky.
Evening Star,
bright as a lantern in the window.

The exiled ones are returning.
The haggard King.
The savvy Queen.
The broken-hearted Jester.

No company from dying wasps,
but their sovereign venom is in effect;
a catalyst to hear the song
of the wind that sings our vespers.

About the Author

Ben Patrick Holden is a writer from the South Pennines, now living with his wife, son and daughter by the woods in the North of England.

For stories, essays, poetry, and other writing, visit:

www.benpholden.com

Thank you for reading.

Printed in Great Britain
by Amazon

87017511R00038